Mapping Global Issues

Endangered Species

Peter Littlewood

FRANKLIN WATTS
LONDON • SYDNEY

First published in 2011 by Franklin Watts

Copyright © 2011 Arcturus Publishing Limited

Franklin Watts
338 Euston Road
London NW1 3BH

Franklin Watts Australia
Level 17/207 Kent Street, Sydney, NSW 2000

Produced by Arcturus Publishing Limited, 26/27 Bickels Yard, 151–153 Bermondsey Street, London SE1 3HA

The right of Peter Littlewood to be identified as the author of this work has been asserted by him in accordance with the Copyright, Designs and Patents Act 1988.

Series concept: Alex Woolf
Editor and picture researcher: Alex Woolf
Designer: Jane Hawkins
Map illustrator: Stefan Chabluk

Picture credits
Corbis: 10 (Atlantide Phototravel), 30 (Michael & Patricia Fogden), 42–43 (Dan Guravich).
Jutzi, Michael: 31.
Nature Picture Library: 35 (David Fleetham), 39 (Nick Gordon).
Science Photo Library: 7 (Mark Garlick).
Shutterstock: 19 (Uryadnikov Sergey), 21 (Mike Flippo), 22 (FloridaStock), 27 (Arkady Mazor), 41 (Eric Gevaert).

Every attempt has been made to clear copyright. Should there be any inadvertent omission, please apply to the publisher for rectification.

Cover picture: The orang-utan is a critically endangered species of primate that lives on the islands of Borneo and Sumatra.

Map sources
9 (Artificial Habitat), 13 (www.seaworld.org), 15 (Save the Tiger Fund), 17 (based on William Temple Hornaday's late-19th-century research), 25 (US Geological Survey), 29 (WWF), 33 (Florida Museum of Natural History), 37 (National Oceanic and Atmospheric Administration).

A CIP catalogue record for this book is available from the British Library.

Dewey Decimal Classification Number: 333.9'522

ISBN 978 1 4451 0514 7
SL001632EN
Supplier 03, Date 0911, Print Run 1035

Printed in China

Franklin Watts is a division of Hachette Children's Books, an Hachette UK company.
www.hachette.co.uk

Contents

1: A Brief History of Extinction

Death comes to us all. It's the one certainty in life. And one day, in the very distant future, the last human on planet Earth will die. That is, of course, provided we don't destroy ourselves much sooner through our own actions. Extinction – the total dying out of a species of plant or animal – can be a natural process. Maybe the climate changes over time to create conditions that a species cannot survive. Perhaps a new, better adapted and more successful species gradually evolves and pushes out an older one. Sometimes a particular species is just too tasty and can't run very fast!

CASE STUDY

A PLANETARY WHODUNNIT!

About 65 million years ago, at the end of the Cretaceous Period, something happened on Earth that destroyed an entire type of animal life: the dinosaurs. All of the dinosaurs disappeared from the fossil record during a period of around a million years or less, having dominated the planet for the previous 165 million years. What could have caused this catastrophic extinction? There are several possible answers:

- The 'volcano theory' proposes that a big increase in volcanic eruptions threw enormous quantities of ash and poisonous gases into the atmosphere, suffocating the dinosaurs.

- The 'impact theory' suggests that the Earth was hit by a massive asteroid, perhaps 10 kilometres across. Clay rich in the mineral iridium, which is rare on Earth but often present in meteorites, is found across the world in the rock strata (layers) from the late Cretaceous Period, supporting this theory. The impact of a huge asteroid would have sent enormous clouds of dust and ash into the atmosphere causing rapid global cooling and permanent darkness. This would have killed many plants and, in turn, caused plant-eating dinosaurs to starve to death.

- Another theory is that a disease arrived on the planet that killed all the dinosaurs – a kind of dino-plague!

An asteroid some 10 kilometres across may have hit the Earth's oceans 65 million years ago. Water vapour thrown into the atmosphere by the impact would have lowered global temperatures, perhaps causing the extinction of the dinosaurs.

The human threat

One species has grown in numbers at an alarming rate, causing many others to become endangered or extinct. It has robbed other plants and animals of their habitats (the type of environment they like to live in), hunted or harvested them to extinction, and caused pollution on a scale that has endangered or wiped out other, more sensitive species. It has even altered the planet's climate! What could this destructive species be? Is it some kind of monster? Well, no: it's *Homo sapiens sapiens*. It's us, people. In the last few centuries alone, we have pushed hundreds, if not thousands of other species to extinction and we have endangered thousands more.

Prehistoric extinction

Modern humans, with all of our technological advances, are much more threatening to other species than we used to be. But when we look back at our ancestors, we can see how our destructive habits have a very long history.

Take the woolly mammoth, for example. According to the fossil record, these animals first appeared across what is now Europe and Asia about 300,000 years ago. At that time the world was in the grip of an ice age. The climate was generally much colder than it is today. The mammoths, with their thick, woolly coats, were well adapted to living in the icy conditions of the time. They were herbivores, eating grasses, sedges and twigs.

Mammoths thrived for about 280,000 years, reaching a peak in population about 42,000 years ago, when glacier coverage was at its greatest. But then, as the planet gradually warmed up, their numbers began to decline. By about 6,000 years ago, their habitat had shrunk to just 10 per cent of what it had been at its peak. But it was humans who really sealed the mammoths' fate. The extreme cold of the mammoths' chosen territories had prevented contact with humans, but as the temperatures increased, humans began hunting them. The last mammoth died about 5,000 years ago.

Dead as a dodo

The dodo was a bird that lived on Mauritius, an island in the Indian Ocean, off the coast of Africa. Portuguese sailors discovered the island in 1598. If they hadn't, there's a good chance that the dodo would still be alive today. From descriptions and illustrations of the time, we know that the dodo was a grey, turkey-sized bird, with a big beak and a fluffy white plume of feathers on its tail. It had little stubby wings, useless for flying – but it didn't need to fly, as it had no predators.

When the sailors landed on the island, they were amazed that these birds were not at all frightened and didn't try to run away as humans walked up to them. They named them 'dodo', which means 'stupid' in Portuguese! Dodos didn't realize that humans were dangerous, so the sailors found them very easy to kill for food. The dodo made its nest on the ground. Dodo eggs and chicks were trampled on and eaten by the rats, pigs and monkeys that had been transported on the ships. Within a few years of their discovery, there were very few dodos left. By 1681 they were extinct.

PERSPECTIVES

KILLER INSTINCT

When the sailors first landed in Mauritius and saw the gentle dodos, it never occurred to them to do anything other than to club them to death.... Presumably, hitting defenceless, tame, flightless birds over the head with a club was just something to do.

Richard Dawkins, *The God Delusion*, 2006

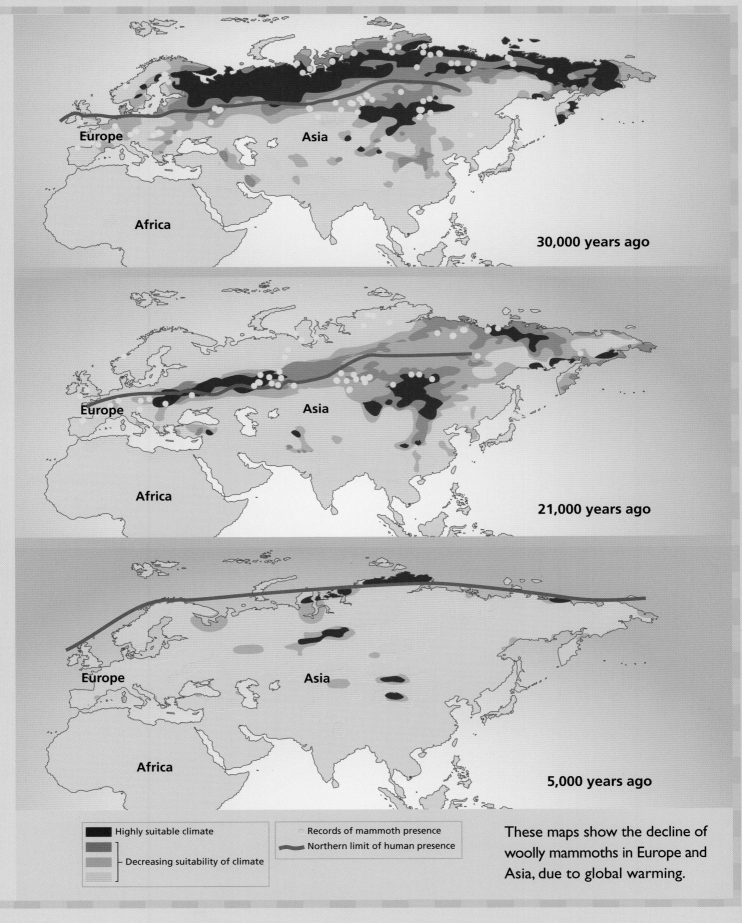

Europe

Asia

Africa

30,000 years ago

Europe

Asia

Africa

21,000 years ago

Europe

Asia

Africa

5,000 years ago

■ Highly suitable climate

▯ Decreasing suitability of climate

▫ Records of mammoth presence

━ Northern limit of human presence

These maps show the decline of woolly mammoths in Europe and Asia, due to global warming.

This monk in Thailand is helping to care for a tiger that has been injured by poachers at Wa Pa Luangta Bua, the 'Tiger Temple'.

Monitoring endangered species

An endangered species is one in which the number of remaining individuals has become so low that it is in danger of extinction. A species becomes 'extinct in the wild' when it has not been seen in the wild for at least 50 years. It can only be classed as fully extinct after the last captive example of the species has died.

With all our technological advances, we modern humans are better at destroying species than our ancestors, but we are also better at knowing we're doing it. We have become skilled at monitoring the world's species. This has allowed conservation groups to try to protect species when they become endangered and hopefully prevent them from becoming extinct.

The Red List

The International Union for the Conservation of Nature (IUCN) publishes the Red List of endangered species across the planet. The list is based on the evidence of over 1,700 scientists working in 130 countries around the world whose job it is to protect and learn more about rare species. According to the Red List, some 17,300 species of the 47,677 species assessed so far are considered under threat, including 12 per cent of the world's birds, 21 per cent of mammals, 30 per cent of reptiles, 31 per cent of amphibians, 37 per cent of fish and 70 per cent of the world's plants.

Extinction rates

The Red List is likely to be massively underestimating the extent of the problem. This is because it takes a long time to gather data on each species. The gap between official statistics and reality can be seen when one looks at extinctions. As of March 2010, there have been 869 officially recorded extinctions since 1500 CE. A further 208 are listed as 'possibly extinct', meaning that they have not been seen for decades. However, the IUCN has calculated that

between 100 and 1,000 of every million species on the planet are now becoming extinct each year.

Fossil records show that the background rate of extinction (the rate at which it would occur naturally, without human interference) is around one in every million species per year. Alarmingly, the rate of extinction that we humans are causing is similar to that experienced by the dinosaurs. That means we're as effective at wiping out species as the giant asteroid or dino-plague that took place 65 million years ago!

FACTS and FIGURES

TEEMING WITH LIFE – AND DEATH

There are 1.8 million known and scientifically named species on Earth. Only 41,000 of these have been assessed by the IUCN's panel of scientists. However, it is believed that there could be up to 30 million species in existence on Earth. And this is only about 3 per cent of all species ever to have lived on Earth.

Source: IUCN

The current rate of extinctions is at least 100 times the background rate, but some estimates suggest it is as much as 10,000 times the background rate! If present rates continue, half of all species on Earth could be extinct by 2100.

Edward O Wilson, Harvard biologist, 2007

2: Hunting and Poaching

Unlike our mammoth-hunting ancestors, most people today get their food from farms. So why does hunting continue? Hunters argue that they help maintain healthy populations of wild animals, and a skilful hunter can ensure the kill is swift. The Inuit hunt seals for food and clothing. They claim they hunt humanely and without endangering the seal population. The problem is that not all hunters behave responsibly. Animals can endure lingering, painful deaths, and hunting has brought some species to the brink of extinction.

Gorillas

Gorillas, our closest relatives after chimpanzees, are now standing on the cliff-edge of extinction, and we're getting ready to push them off. As of February 2010, there were only about 680 mountain gorillas left in the wild. They live in two regions in Central Africa, just 45 kilometres apart. They are the Bwindi Impenetrable National Park in Uganda and the mountainous Virungas region, which straddles the borders of Rwanda and the Democratic Republic of Congo (DRC).

The situation is slightly better for western lowland gorillas, but they are still classified on the Red List as 'critically endangered'. Their population has fallen by 80 per cent in just three generations, and there are currently thought to be about 100,000 to 125,000 of them left in the wild, spread across a huge territory. Their dense and often impenetrable forest habitat makes it difficult to calculate their true numbers.

The gorilla meat trade

Gorillas have become endangered because they are hunted for their meat. This may seem hard to understand, but in the DRC, cattle and chicken meat is not plentiful, and is too expensive for many people. It actually makes economic sense for people to venture deep into the rainforest and hunt gorillas. The prices they obtain for gorilla meat make it worthwhile. A hand-sized piece of pre-cut and smoked gorilla meat costs about US$6. Customers can even buy gorilla hands for about US$6 each!

CLOSE RELATION

No one who looks into a gorilla's eyes — intelligent, gentle, vulnerable — can remain unchanged, for the gap between ape and human vanishes; we know that the gorilla still lives within us.

George B Schaller, in *National Geographic*, October 1995

An undercover investigation, conducted by the conservation group Endangered Species International (ESI), which took place in the Kouilou region of the DRC in 2009, found that at least two gorillas per week, out of a population of about 200, are being killed and sold as bushmeat there. That means 50 per cent of the population is being killed in one year. At that rate, gorillas could be extinct in the region in less than ten years.

This is the story in just one area of the DRC, but it is likely that gorillas are being killed at similar rates across many parts of their range. At the moment gorillas receive very little protection. Although there are laws in place to protect them from hunters, little is done to enforce these laws, so the

This map shows the ranges of the western lowland and mountain gorillas.

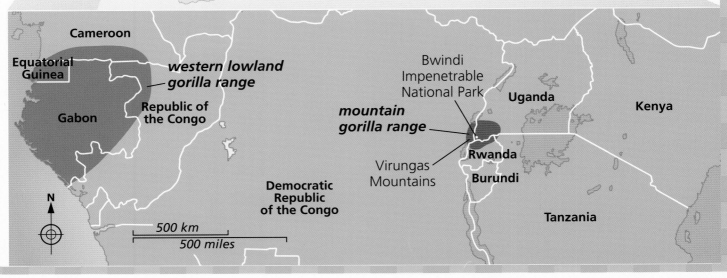

Cameroon

Equatorial Guinea

western lowland gorilla range

Gabon

Republic of the Congo

Bwindi Impenetrable National Park

mountain gorilla range

Uganda

Kenya

Rwanda

Virungas Mountains

Burundi

Democratic Republic of the Congo

N

500 km

500 miles

Tanzania

hunting continues. For now, the gorillas are protected to some extent by the remoteness of their habitats. Yet people are encroaching ever deeper into the forests, looking for food and firewood.

The ivory trade

The African elephant is so badly threatened by poaching that it could be extinct in just 15 years. In 2009 the elephant population was 600,000, but this was decreasing by 38,000 each year. Many more elephants are dying each year than are born. This is in spite of an international ban on the trade of ivory (the substance elephants' tusks are made of) in force since 1990.

Ivory is used to make many kinds of ornaments and jewellery and is highly valued in East Asia. Although it is illegal to buy and sell ivory products, the trade seems to be growing. In 2010 a kilogram of ivory was worth around US$6,200. And as a pair of male elephant tusks may weigh over 200 kilograms, it is easy to see how money can be made by poaching elephants.

The trade is continuing almost unchecked throughout Central and West Africa. For example, Zakouma National Park in Chad had 3,885 elephants in 2005. By 2009 there were just 617. In the same time period, 11 rangers (men whose job it is to protect the elephants) were shot by poachers. Tragically, only the tusks are taken by the poachers. The rest of the elephant is just left to rot where it falls.

Tigers in danger

According to the World Wildlife Fund (WWF), in 2010 there are just 3,200 to 3,500 tigers left in the wild – that is the total number on Earth! In 1900 there were over 100,000 of them. The main reasons for their decline are:
- loss of habitat
- coming into conflict with humans and livestock and consequently being killed
- being targeted by hunters for the illegal trade in tiger parts.

Take your tiger pills!

Tiger parts are thought to have all kinds of health-giving properties in Chinese medicine. The medicines are of questionable value: tiger whiskers are supposed to cure toothache; a tiger's nose, if hung over a marriage bed, apparently increases the chances of having a boy; and tiger bone wine (worth US$240 for 500 millilitres) cures arthritis and rheumatism. A single wild tiger, sold on the black market

PERSPECTIVES

DESPERATE MEASURES

Many African countries are suffering terrible drought and local people are desperate. Killing elephants brings money, alas.

Heather Sohl, WWF

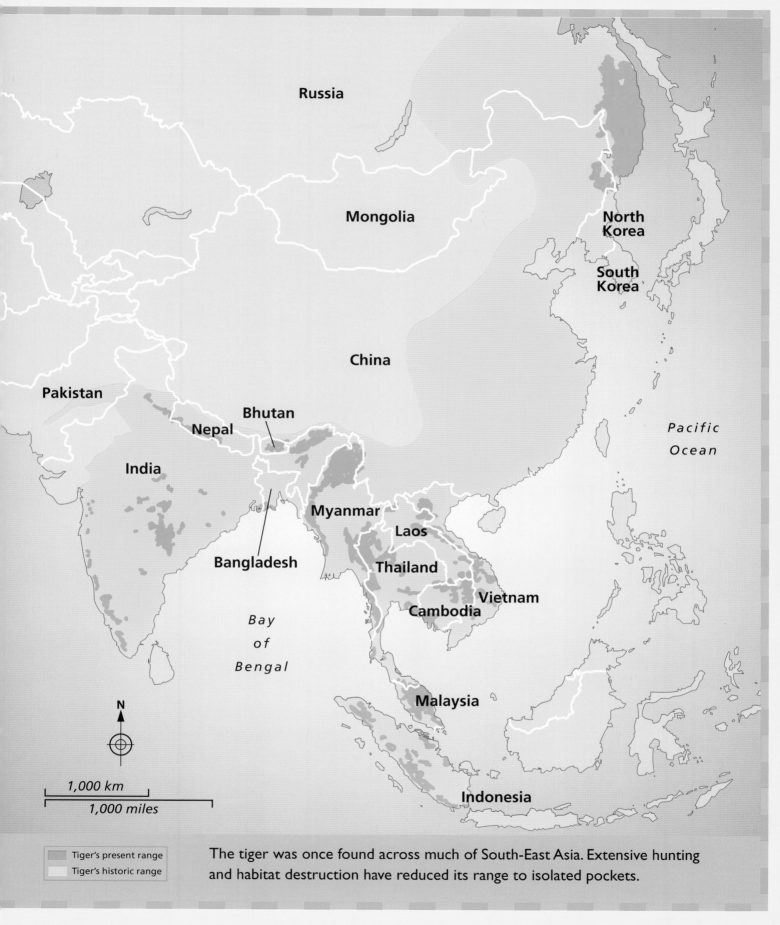

Russia

Mongolia

North
Korea

South
Korea

Pakistan

*Pacific
Ocean*

China

Bhutan

Nepal

India

Myanmar

Laos

Bangladesh

Thailand

Vietnam

Cambodia

*Bay
of
Bengal*

N

Malaysia

1,000 km

1,000 miles

Indonesia

Tiger's present range
Tiger's historic range

The tiger was once found across much of South-East Asia. Extensive hunting and habitat destruction have reduced its range to isolated pockets.

for 'parts' can be worth up to US$50,000. It is easy to see how a poor farmer, expecting to make just a few hundred dollars a year to feed himself and his family, is likely to be tempted by the rewards of hunting a tiger.

Buffalo

In the 1600s an estimated 50 to 60 million buffalo (or North American bison) roamed the plains of North America. They were hunted by Native Americans for centuries, but this had little impact on such an enormous population. The Native Americans used almost all parts of the buffalo they killed. The meat was eaten. Hides were made into moccasins, leggings and other clothing, tipi covers and carrying cases. Fur was woven into ropes or used for stuffing. Hooves were boiled up to make glue, and horns were used to make arrow points, ladles, spoons and cups. Even buffalo dung was utilized as fuel or as a stone polish!

In the 1800s, European settlers saw the value of the buffalo as a source of food, clothing and raw materials. A high-quality buffalo hide was worth US$50 and even an average one was worth US$3 – at a time when a labourer's wages were around US$1 a day. Mass hunting using powerful hunting rifles reduced buffalo numbers at an alarming rate. The hunters used the buffalo hides for leather or to make thick winter coats. They also took their tongues, which were considered a delicacy. The carcasses were then left to rot on the plains. When all that remained were the bones, these were gathered up and shipped via rail for processing into fertilizer.

PERSPECTIVES

RUTHLESS SLAUGHTER

Thirty years ago millions of the great unwieldy animals existed on this continent. Innumerable droves roamed, comparatively undisturbed and unmolested.... Many thousands have been ruthlessly and shamefully slain every season for the past twenty years or more by white hunters and tourists merely for their robes, and in sheer wanton sport, and their huge carcasses left to fester and rot, and their bleached skeletons to strew the deserts and lonely plains.

'In the Prime of the Buffalo' by J F Baltimore.
The Overland Monthly and Out West Magazine,
November 1889

Back from the brink

By 1890 there were probably fewer than 2,000 buffalo left in the whole of North America. By this time, when it was almost too late, people realized that the buffalo needed protecting if it was to survive. Thanks to careful conservation and captive breeding, there are now around 500,000 buffalo in North America, living on around 4,000 privately owned ranches. They are bred for their meat, which is low in fat and

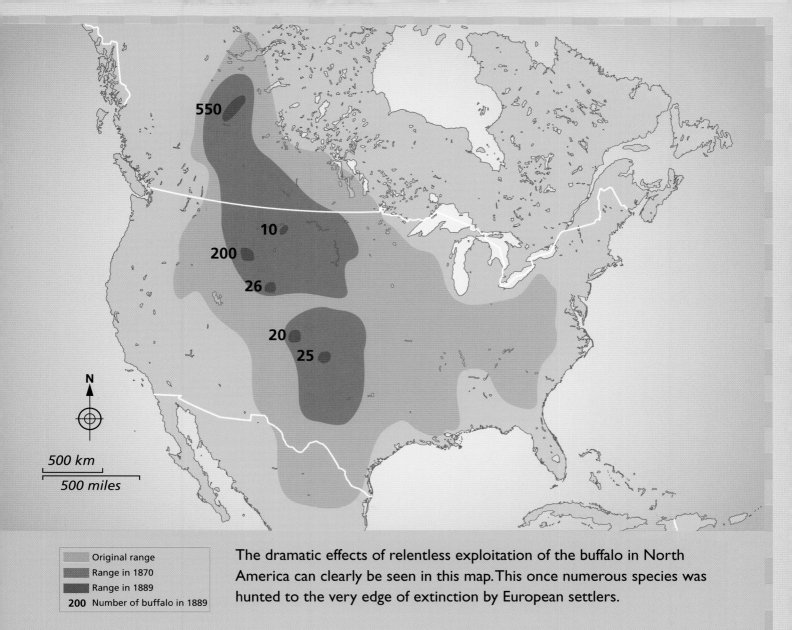

550

10

200

26

20

25

500 km

500 miles

N

Original range
Range in 1870
Range in 1889
200 Number of buffalo in 1889

The dramatic effects of relentless exploitation of the buffalo in North America can clearly be seen in this map. This once numerous species was hunted to the very edge of extinction by European settlers.

high in protein, making it a good choice for the health conscious. There are still very few truly wild buffalo in North America. In fact, the Red List estimates that there are just 15,000 across the whole continent.

In the case of the buffalo, humans realized what they were doing just in time. This should give us some cause for hope. If the buffalo can be brought back from the brink of extinction, we may be able to save other species in the same way. We will look again at how we can save species in danger of extinction in Chapter 6.

3: Habitat Loss, Pollution and Invaders

As one of the most adaptable species on the planet, humans are able to survive in all kinds of conditions, from the frozen wastes of the Arctic to the dry heat of the Sahara. We do this by making things to help us, like thermal clothing and sun block, but also by changing the landscape to suit our purposes: clearing forests for timber and farmland, for example. Unfortunately, in making these changes, we often endanger animal and plant species that depend on these habitats for survival.

All change

The majority of animal and plant species are far less adaptable than humans. They have evolved over millions of years in a particular environment and are superbly adapted to those conditions. When the conditions change, they struggle to survive. This often causes a chain reaction. If one creature dies out, so do the predators that depend on it for their survival, and so on up the food chain. And it's not just changes to the landscape that can threaten the animals and plants of a particular habitat. Other human-caused threats include pollution and the introduction of new species.

'Man of the forest'

The orang-utan is one of our closest relatives, sharing 96.4 per cent of our DNA. Its name even means 'man of the forest' in the Malay language. Orang-utans used to live across a huge swathe of South-East Asian rainforest, stretching from southern China to the foothills of the Himalayas and south to Java. Today they survive only on the Indonesian islands of Borneo and Sumatra.

FACTS and FIGURES

DECLINE DUE TO DEFORESTATION

Just a century ago, the combined orang-utan population of Borneo and Sumatra was around 230,000. In 2010 orang-utans on the two islands number no more than 62,500. In the last ten years alone, their numbers have fallen by up to 50 per cent. It's easy to see why. In just 20 years, between 1990 and 2010, about 80 per cent of suitable habitat has been destroyed. Of the remaining forest, only 2 per cent is properly protected.

Source: WWF UK, 2010

Almost human: it is easy to see the intelligence in the eyes of this mother orang-utan and her baby. Tragically, this species is now under threat of extinction and could disappear from Borneo's wild forests by 2020.

The IUCN Red List of 2007 classifies Bornean orang-utans as endangered and Sumatran orang-utans as critically endangered. The main threats to the orang-utan's survival come from commercial logging (much of which is illegal) and land clearance for agriculture and the creation of plantations. A 2007 United Nations Environment Programme (UNEP) report suggested that 98 per cent of Indonesia's rainforests may be destroyed by 2022. If this happens it would mean the end of the orang-utan.

Here today, gone tomorrow?

The Bornean clouded leopard is a medium-sized wild cat that shares the orang-utan's home in the rainforests of Borneo and Sumatra. In 2007 it was discovered to be a separate species from the clouded leopard that lives in mainland China. Despite its name, it is not a leopard, but a type of wild cat. It gets its name from the oval-shaped markings on its coat, which are said to resemble clouds.

The Bornean clouded leopard weighs up to 25 kilograms and uses its agility to hunt at ground level. Its canine teeth are over 5 centimetres long – longer than those of any other big cat and only exceeded relative to its body size by the sabre-toothed tiger of prehistoric times. As Bornean clouded leopards live deep in the rainforests and are habitually secretive, it is very difficult to know for sure how many there are left. According to the most optimistic estimates, there are 11,000 left in Borneo and 7,000 in Sumatra.

CASE STUDY

SHOULD WE PANDER TO THE PANDA?

The giant panda, which lives in the mountains of Sichuan, Shaanxi and Gansu provinces of central China, is recognized worldwide as a symbol for conservation. It is regarded by the IUCN as a 'conservation-reliant endangered species', meaning that it is dependent on human efforts for its survival. There are certainly no more than 3,000 left in the wild. Most of these live in 40 reserves in central China.

During the late 1940s, China's rapidly expanding population caused a growing demand for land and raw materials. As a result, much of the panda's habitat – mountainous forests with thick stands of bamboo – was destroyed. The panda was also hunted for its fur. In the 1950s, when people realized pandas were in danger of dying out, they were often caged to preserve them. But caged pandas failed to reproduce, further endangering the species.

Some conservationists now consider the giant panda to be beyond help. Certainly, it is a species on which a great deal of money has been spent over the last few decades, to little effect. Perhaps it would now be better to let the giant panda fend for itself.

A giant panda feeds on bamboo in its mountainous forest home. This iconic symbol for the conservation movement is only able to survive thanks to human intervention.

The bald eagle, the national symbol of the United States, was driven to the brink of extinction by farmers' use of DDT as a pesticide.

A twin threat

Like the orang-utans, the Bornean clouded leopard is threatened by habitat destruction. In addition, it is hunted, despite being a protected species. It is hunted for its pelt (skin), as well as its other parts. The bones and teeth of Bornean clouded leopards are thought to have healing properties in Chinese medicine. Threatened by hunters and habitat destruction, this wild cat could be extinct in the wild by 2022 – along with the orang-utan. If that happens the Bornean clouded leopard would have disappeared just 15 years after humans realized it existed as a distinct species!

Pollution

Animals can become endangered for lots of reasons. Hunting and habitat destruction are highly visible causes. Less visible, but equally destructive, is pollution from factory waste and agriculture. For example, the bumblebee bat of Thailand and Myanmar – the world's smallest mammal

– is threatened by pollution from cement factories in Myanmar.

DDT and birds of prey

Sometimes, people have used chemicals on the land without realizing the consequences. In the the 1950s, a chemical called DDT was introduced to farming. It was a pesticide, and was highly effective in controlling insect pests. No one realized at the time that DDT was bioaccumulative in its effects. In other words, it became concentrated in the fatty tissues of many species of animal that were exposed to it.

DDT got into the waterways, affecting the zooplankton, tiny creatures that are present in open water. Fish would eat the zooplankton, accumulating DDT in their own bodies. Birds of prey, such as the osprey, then ate the fish, which gave them large doses of DDT. On the land, DDT found its way into earthworms and other minibeasts, which were eaten by small birds such as robins, which in turn were eaten by birds of prey like eagles.

The DDT did not kill the birds of prey, but it affected the way their bodies metabolized calcium. As a result, their eggs had thinner, weaker shells, which would collapse under the adult bird while it sat on them in the nest. The use of DDT brought many species of bird of prey to the brink of extinction, both in the UK and United States. For example, there were thought to be as many as 500,000 bald eagles in the United States

in the 1700s. By the mid-1950s there were just 412 breeding pairs in the whole country. The use of DDT was banned in the United States in 1972 and in the UK in 1984. Bird of prey numbers have recovered as a result.

Otters

European otters are beautiful, secretive creatures – graceful swimmers and lethal hunters. They used to be plentiful in the UK's rivers, but by the 1970s they had almost disappeared. This was due to the pollution of Britain's waterways by chemicals used in the manufacture of pesticides and electrical equipment. The chemicals bioaccumulated and affected the otter's ability to reproduce, with the result that the species almost became extinct across much of its range.

Since 1993, when an initiative was launched to clean up the UK's rivers, the otter has returned. Legislation banning or restricting the use of damaging chemicals across much of Europe has, according to conservationists, led to the otter's gradual recovery. However, the IUCN still classifies it as 'near threatened'.

Alien invaders

In the case of pollution, we have seen how human actions can have unintended consequences for plants and animals. Another example of this is the introduction of a species to a country or region where it has not existed before.

This is what happened in the case of the rhododendron, a shrub-like plant that grows naturally in the Himalayas. It was introduced into the UK in the 1700s and by Victorian times it was a popular garden plant. The problem is that there is almost nothing in the UK that eats rhododendron, and it is capable of spreading rapidly. It shades the ground beneath it, making it impossible for native wild flowers to grow.

Why squirrels have turned grey!

The grey squirrel was introduced to the UK from North America in the 19th century as a curiosity to add interest to parks. No one predicted how successful this species would be, and how damaging to the native red squirrel. There is some evidence to suggest that grey squirrels carry the parapox virus, which is harmless to them, but deadly to red squirrels. This put reds at a disadvantage whenever the species met.

Since grey squirrels are larger, stronger and more disease-resistant than reds, they were able to out-compete them. Grey squirrels prefer broadleaf woodlands. As a result, the red squirrels have retreated mainly to the coniferous forests of the north of England and Scotland – although a couple of isolated populations continue to exist in southern England and Wales. There are now an estimated 2.5 million grey squirrels in England and Wales, and fewer than 140,000 reds.

The nutria: from fur to fear

The nutria (known in Europe as the coypu) is a large rodent, weighing about 11 kilograms, which was imported to the United States from South America in the 1930s.

CASE STUDY

MARSHLAND IN DANGER

Another unanticipated consequence of the introduction of nutria has been the loss of saltmarsh across Chesapeake Bay in the eastern United States. Between 1970 and 2010, up to 2,800 hectares of saltmarsh were lost as a result of overfeeding by nutria. The nutria likes to eat the roots and tubers of marsh-growing plants, such as bulrushes. The roots act as a glue, holding together the sediment that makes up the fragile soil of the saltmarshes. When the roots are removed, the sediment washes away easily, making it difficult for plants to regrow.

Nutria population established due to escape or release

Nutria range expansion

Nutria never established

Nutria extinct

Source of nutria population unknown

No data available

This map shows how the nutria spread across the United States, having escaped or been released from farms in the southern states, along with Washington and Oregon.

Nutria were farmed for their fur, which was used in the expanding fur trade. During the 1940s, the market for fur collapsed and with it the nutria farms. Many farmers simply turned their nutria loose. Nutria are more aggressive than the native muskrat and they reproduce rapidly. The nutria population in one isolated region of around 4,000 hectares in Dorchester County, Maryland, has increased from 150 in 1968 to around 50,000 today! As a result of this invasion, muskrats have been forced out.

4: The Effects of Climate Change

The term 'climate change' means an alteration to long-term global weather patterns. This could include a change in average global temperatures, as well as increased instances of drought, storms and flooding. At the moment, the Earth's climate is gradually becoming warmer, so climate change is often referred to as 'global warming'. While there are a few scientists who doubt that human actions are responsible for climate change, the vast majority agree that we are contributing to changes in our planet's climate. And this, in turn, is having a major impact on the planet's animals and plants.

Adaptation

Animal and plant species are capable of adapting to changes in climate. Some do this gradually, by physical adaptation. For example, the huge ears of the fennec fox are a physical adaptation to the changing conditions in the Sahara, where the fennec fox lives. The ears act rather like a car's radiator, filling with blood which is then able to cool, thus dispersing excess heat from the fox's body. Thousands of years ago, as the Sahara became hotter, some ancestors of the fennec fox that were born with larger ears found it easier to survive in the new conditions. Over the years, the bigger-eared individuals were more successful and mated with each other, leading to the birth of even bigger-eared foxes, which were even better suited to the climate.

Migration

Sometimes animals are able to adapt by migrating to areas where the climate is more suitable for them. Swallows, for example, spend the winter in the southern hemisphere, then migrate to the northern hemisphere in the summer. They travel thousands of kilometres each year to find the warmest weather – rather like humans going on their holidays!

Dangers of climate change

But what happens when changes to the climate happen too fast for species to adapt to through evolution, or when species are hemmed into their current range by physical barriers such as seas, mountain ranges or human settlement? As we shall see, that is when species can become

Each of these cows is releasing up to 200 litres of methane every day. Methane is over 20 times more powerful than carbon dioxide as a greenhouse gas.

CASE STUDY

HUMAN CAUSES OF CLIMATE CHANGE

Humans have contributed to climate change mostly through emissions of carbon dioxide. This is a 'greenhouse gas', which means it is a type of gas that traps the Sun's heat within the Earth's atmosphere (like the glass walls of a greenhouse), helping to warm the planet. We create carbon dioxide by burning fossil fuels (coal, oil and gas). Much of this carbon dioxide is absorbed by the planet's trees in a process called photosynthesis. But because we have chopped down so many trees in the rainforests and other forested areas, less carbon dioxide is being absorbed. We also contribute to climate change by farming cattle on a vast scale. One cow emits up to 200 litres of methane per day. Methane is a powerful greenhouse gas. And with an estimated 1.5 billion cattle alive today, they can make a significant impact.

endangered or even become extinct as a result of climate change.

Polar bears: feeling the heat

Polar bears live within the Arctic Circle, which encompasses parts of Alaska, north-west Canada, Greenland, some parts of

Norway and northern Russia. All of these lands surround the Arctic Ocean. At the centre of the Arctic Ocean is the polar ice cap, an area that extends some 800 kilometres south from the North Pole, and which is always frozen. The rest of the Arctic Ocean freezes only in the winter, when the area of ice more than doubles. On this outer ring of 'pack ice' polar bears like to hunt during the winter months.

As global temperatures have risen over the last few decades, the area of pack ice has decreased. For example, in 2005, the pack ice receded 320 kilometres further than it did in the 1970s. The ice is also much thinner, with an average thickness of 1.8 metres today, compared to 3 metres in the 1950s. Average temperatures on the northern coast of Alaska are around 2°C higher than they were in 1949.

Polar bears like to hunt on the edges of the pack ice, where it is thinner. Here they can catch their favourite food – ringed and bearded seals. Using their excellent sense of smell, they find a seal's breathing hole in the ice. Then they crouch down nearby and wait. When the seal puts its head above water to breathe, the polar bear strikes! Polar bears only need to eat every four to five days, but finding sufficient food on the shrinking pack ice is becoming increasingly difficult.

The big swim

Polar bears also hunt on ice floes – areas of ice that have broken away from the pack ice and which float on the sea. As the ice melts, the bears are forced to swim further to get to new ice. In 1986, about 4 per cent of all polar bears sighted were swimming. By 2005, this had increased to 20 per cent. They are excellent swimmers, so a sea crossing of 30 kilometres is not a problem to them. But increasingly, gaps between ice floes suitable for polar bears to hunt from are widening to 100 kilometres or more. Swims of this length can leave the bears exhausted and vulnerable to hypothermia.

Signs of pressure on the polar bear include instances of cannibalism, where bears have eaten their own cubs! While this is not common, frequency has increased from one or two cases per year to at least eight.

FACTS and FIGURES

A BLEAK FUTURE

The IUCN Red List for 2010 lists polar bears as 'vulnerable'. The IUCN expects polar bear populations to decline by more than 30 per cent in the coming 45 years. Summer sea ice is expected to reduce by 50 to 100 per cent by 2100. Polar bears are thought to be unable to adapt quickly enough to the changed conditions caused by continual climate change and it is likely they will have almost disappeared in the wild within 100 years.

Source: IUCN Red List, February 2010

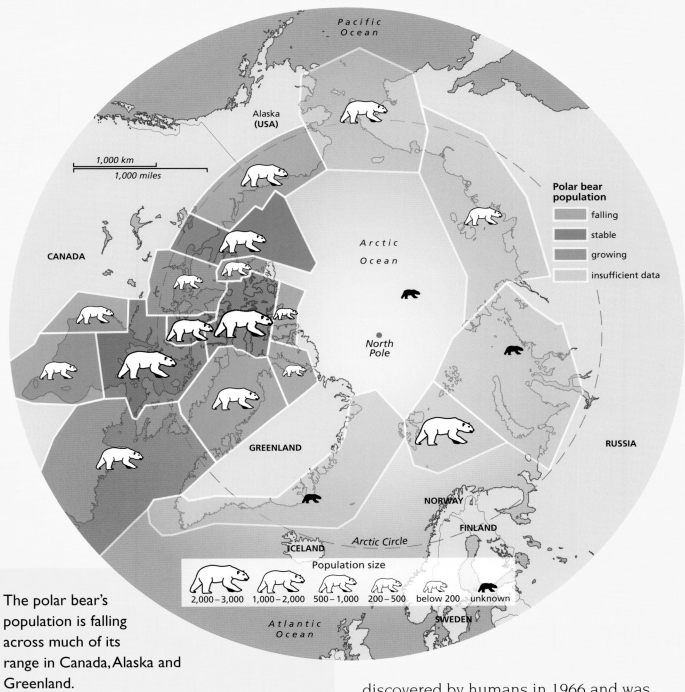

Polar bear population

- falling
- stable
- growing
- insufficient data

1,000 km
1,000 miles

Pacific Ocean

Alaska (USA)

CANADA

Arctic Ocean

North Pole

GREENLAND

RUSSIA

NORWAY

FINLAND

ICELAND

Arctic Circle

Atlantic Ocean

SWEDEN

Population size

2,000–3,000   1,000–2,000   500–1,000   200–500   below 200   unknown

The polar bear's population is falling across much of its range in Canada, Alaska and Greenland.

Climate change: the reason golden toads croaked it?

The golden toad used to live in significant numbers in Costa Rica's Monteverde Cloud Forest Reserve. The species was only discovered by humans in 1966 and was endemic – that is, it could not be found anywhere else in the world.

In 1987 researchers counted several thousand golden toads, which had gathered to breed in pools. Just one year later, only ten golden toads were found and in 1989,

Male golden toads have not been seen in the Monteverde Cloud Forest of Costa Rica since 1989, when a single male was found. They are now classified by the IUCN as extinct.

only one was seen. Since then, no golden toads have been seen and they are now classed by the IUCN as extinct.

So what caused the sudden extinction of a whole species? The cloud forests, high up in the mountains, are often shrouded in mist, which gives them their name and provides the moisture the forest needs during the January to April dry season. Since the 1970s, the frequency of the mists has declined significantly as a result of the warming of the oceans and the atmosphere.

In 1988–89 there was a major El Niño event. El Niño is a climate pattern that occurs about every five years in the tropical Pacific region and causes unusually warm waters on the South American coast. The El Niño event made the climate in Costa Rica particularly warm and dry, conditions that the golden toad may not have been able to survive. The warm conditions may also have helped a fungal disease called chytrid to flourish. Chytrid has been responsible for wiping out many amphibian populations and could well have helped to kill off the golden toad.

The Snowdon lily: clinging to survival

The Snowdon lily is a remnant of the last ice age and it thrives on the high rocky crags of Snowdon in North Wales, where it is well suited to the cold, harsh conditions. However, climate scientists predict that Snowdon may lose its snowcap altogether by 2020 if the climate continues to get warmer at its current rate. This may make the Snowdon lily's survival on the mountain impossible. With warmer temperatures higher up the mountain, other plants will soon start to spread and choke out the last six colonies of Snowdon lilies on the mountain that gives them their name. Then it will be up to colonies in the Alps and Rocky Mountains to ensure the continuation of the species.

With a Welsh population of fewer than 100 bulbs, the Snowdon lily looks set to become the first plant to become extinct in the British Isles as a result of global warming.

5: Oceans in Danger

Humans have eaten fish for thousands of years. For most of that time, humans either weren't numerous enough or lacked the technology to threaten the vast numbers of marine animals in the world's seas and oceans. However, as the human population has expanded, and demand has grown, we have developed ways of catching fish in ever greater numbers. Now there is a real danger that we will wipe out many species.

Atlantic cod

The Atlantic cod was added to a list of endangered species by WWF in 2000, and in 2010 Greenpeace International added the Atlantic cod to its Seafood Red List. This is a list of fish commonly sold in supermarkets around the world, all of which have a very high risk of being sourced from unsustainable fisheries. That is, they have been caught in areas of the ocean that have been overfished. In these areas, the fish are being caught in such quantities that they can no longer replace their numbers through breeding, and the population declines.

Arguments about quotas

Countries that fish for Atlantic cod, including the UK, the United States and Canada, have imposed quotas on their fishermen, limiting the amount of fish they are allowed to catch each year. It is debatable whether these quotas are low enough to ensure the cod's survival. More distressingly, once fishermen reach their annual quota for a particular species, they must throw back any more fish of that species they catch during the rest of the year. In this way, thousands of tonnes of fish are caught and, once dead, are then wastefully thrown back into the sea.

The fishermen argue that they have to make a living and many are urging quotas to be increased. However, if the quotas are raised, it reduces the chances of there being enough cod left in the sea to replenish stocks for the following year. By overfishing, the fishermen could ultimately bring about the end of their industry by driving species like the cod to extinction.

North Atlantic Ocean

Mediterranean Sea

Pacific Ocean

Pacific Ocean

Gulf of Mexico

Indian Ocean

South Atlantic Ocean

N

4,000 km
4,000 miles

The shaded area on the map shows the bluefin tuna's range. While the area may seem large, the chances of encountering bluefin tuna has decreased significantly, due to overfishing.

CASE STUDY

BLUEFIN TUNA

Bluefin tuna can grow to 3 metres in length and weigh up to 650 kilograms. It is used extensively for the Japanese dish sushi, and 75 per cent of all bluefin tuna is eaten in Japan. The fish has become very valuable, with a single fish selling for more than US$120,000 in Japan in January 2010.

There are three separate bluefin tuna populations: two in the Atlantic Ocean and one, the southern bluefin tuna, in the Indian and Pacific oceans. Stocks of all three have declined very rapidly in recent decades. Although the

IUCN does not have up-to-date information on the bluefin tuna, it classifies the Eastern Atlantic stock as 'endangered', the Western Atlantic stock as 'critically endangered' and the southern bluefin tuna also as 'critically endangered'.

Conservationists argue that urgent action is required to limit the fishing of this species, or there is a real danger that it will not recover. In March 2010, at a meeting of the Convention on International Trade in Endangered Species (CITES) (see page 38), Monaco attempted to ban international trade in Atlantic bluefin tuna, but this proposal was rejected.

Whaling

Whales have been hunted for many centuries. There is archaeological evidence from the North Atlantic to show that the Inuit were killing whales as early as 3000 BCE. They did so to feed their families, and a single whale would last a long time. This kind of hunting posed no threat to the whale population.

Industrial whaling

By the 1800s a whaling industry had built up around Antarctica, where whales were plentiful. Many different whales migrated there during the southern hemisphere's summer to feed on the immense swarms of krill that gathered around the Antarctic coast. Many different products were made from whale parts. Whale oils were regarded as among the purest in the world and they were used in lighting and as lubricants for delicate machinery. Baleen was also highly prized. This is the filtering structure in the mouths of most species of whale, which they use to sieve small animals such as krill from large mouthfuls of water. Baleen was used to create items such as carriage springs, fishing rods and hoops for ladies' skirts.

In 1868 a Norwegian called Svend Foyn invented the exploding harpoon. This was a large spear-like weapon, which was fired from a cannon into the body of a whale. The harpoon was attached by a rope to the ship it was fired from. Once inside the whale's body, the harpoon exploded, killing the whale. As faster, steam-powered ships were developed, keeping up with whales was no longer a problem, and with the exploding harpoon, killing them became a lot easier. Not surprisingly, many whale species were driven close to extinction by the whaling industry.

Blue whale

The population of blue whales dropped from between 200,000 and 300,000 in the early 19th century to just 1,000 or 2,000 by 1966, when the International Whaling Commission (IWC) imposed a worldwide ban on hunting this species. The largest examples caught were 33 metres long and weighed 177 tonnes, making the blue whale the largest animal ever known to have existed. In 2010 the WWF estimated the blue whale population in the Southern Ocean at 2,300, and blue whales are still regarded by the IUCN as 'endangered'. It takes five to 15 years for a blue whale to reach sexual maturity, and they give birth only every two to three years, so it will take a very long time for their numbers to recover.

International whaling ban

Since 1986, there has been a ban on all commercial whaling, and in 1994 the IWC created the Southern Ocean Whale Sanctuary, making all whaling illegal in the Southern Ocean.

However, since the ban was imposed, Japanese whalers have killed over 9,000 whales for 'scientific research' purposes. The meat from the whales is then sold as food in Japan. According to the whalers, the main reason for this research is to investigate the health and population size of whale species, in order to provide evidence that their populations have recovered sufficiently for whale hunting to begin again, albeit with strict limits on catch sizes. In 2010 the IWC came under renewed pressure from Japan, Norway and Iceland – the three leading whaling nations – to lift the ban on whaling. It may only be a matter of time before commercial whaling is resumed.

The blue whale is the world's largest animal – of this or any other time in the Earth's history. Its heart weighs around 600 kilograms and its tongue weighs up to 2.7 tonnes!

Antarctic krill – an endangered species?

Krill are tiny, shrimp-like crustaceans that live in all of the world's oceans. Antarctic krill live in the Southern Ocean and, at 5 centimetres long, are the largest of all krill species. They feed on phytoplankton (microscopic plants that live in the sea), which are abundant in the Antarctic.

The world's population of Antarctic krill would fill a football stadium 1,500 times, so how can they possibly be under threat? Believe it or not, their numbers have declined by up to 80 per cent since the 1970s, according to National Geographic.

Scientists believe that the main cause of this decline is climate change. Average temperatures in the Antarctic have risen by 2.5°C in the last 50 years. This means there is now less sea ice and so fewer places where ice algae, on which the Antarctic krill feed, can grow. Less pack ice also means fewer cave-like structures in the ice, which krill need for shelter in the early stages of their development.

The decline in the krill population is very bad news for the Antarctic ecosystem as a whole, as krill provides food for many larger creatures, including baleen whales, squid, penguins and crabeater seals. In fact, you could see Antarctic krill as the foundation for life in the Southern Ocean. If they disappear, then the species that live above them in the food pyramid will also tumble and fall.

Coral

Coral reefs are unique underwater ecosystems, which are home to a quarter of all the world's known marine life. Corals are made up of polyps, tiny living creatures that join together to form colonies. The polyps' skeletons are made of white calcium carbonate, yet corals are very colourful – they can be red, orange, yellow, green, pink, blue and purple. They get their colour from colonies of tiny, single-celled plants called zooxanthellae. Corals feed off the zooxanthellae, obtaining 90 per cent of their energy from them. In return, they give the zooxanthellae the protection, shelter, nutrients and carbon dioxide they need to survive. This is called a symbiotic relationship, because both sides benefit.

Corals are very sensitive to increases in temperature. Higher water temperatures and greater light intensity, even for periods of just eight weeks, can kill the zooxanthellae, causing the coral to starve. The coral becomes 'bleached' – a white, lifeless skeleton.

Australia's Great Barrier Reef is a vast coral reef. At over 2,300 kilometres in length, it is the world's largest living structure. It is home to 400 species of coral and 1,500 species of fish, along with 30 species of whale and dolphin and six species of turtle. In 1998 and 2002, the Great Barrier Reef experienced bleaching events. The first killed 42 per cent and second 54 per cent of its coral.

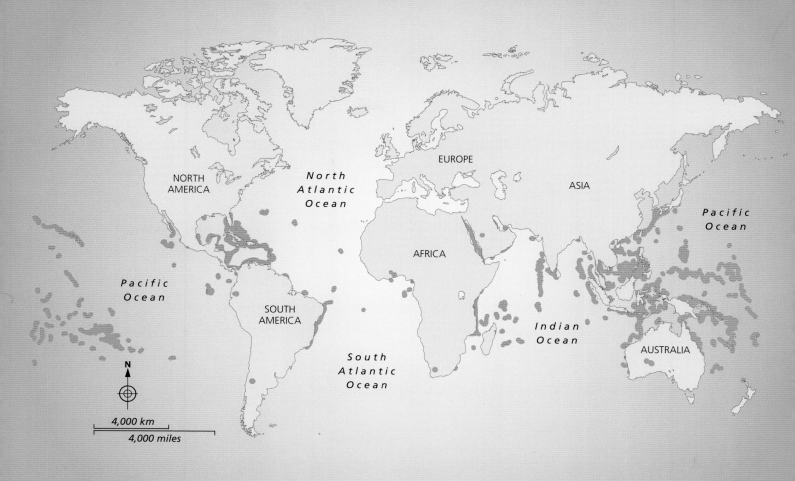

NORTH
AMERICA

North
Atlantic
Ocean

EUROPE

ASIA

Pacific
Ocean

Pacific
Ocean

AFRICA

SOUTH
AMERICA

Indian
Ocean

AUSTRALIA

South
Atlantic
Ocean

N

4,000 km
4,000 miles

This map shows the location of the world's coral reefs. All are located in tropical waters. Seventy per cent of coral reefs could be destroyed by 2050 if global temperatures continue to rise at current rates.

Most areas have since recovered from these events. However, based on conservative estimates for climate change provided by the Intergovernmental Panel on Climate Change (IPCC), by 2100 coral around the world will suffer regular bleaching events in the summertime.

PERSPECTIVES

REEFS IN DANGER

Coral reefs are incredibly important to ocean health ... but if we don't act, we could lose 70 per cent of reefs worldwide by the middle of the century.

Stephanie Wear, the Nature Conservancy's coral expert, from *Time* magazine, 29 August 2010

6: Solutions

The previous chapters have shown that, as a species, humans have been pretty good at threatening or even wiping out other species. This has happened through deliberate acts, such as hunting or overfishing, or as a by-product of our activities, such as pollution or deforestation. So is it all bad news? Are human beings the ultimate destroyers of life on Earth? Well, the news is – thankfully – not all bad. In fact, there are plenty of people who have devoted their lives to preserving the species we share our planet with. And there are plenty more who are working to reduce the impacts that our activities have on other species around the globe.

CITES

The Convention on International Trade in Endangered Species of Wild Fauna and Flora (or CITES for short) is an international agreement between governments, which came into force in 1975. It currently offers varying degrees of protection to around 33,000 species of animal and plant. The purpose of CITES is to prevent countries from buying and selling goods that have originated from endangered species – for example, elephant ivory and tiger parts. Only one species under CITES' protection has so far become extinct in the wild. This is the Spix's macaw. However, its numbers were already so low before CITES came into force that its demise was probably inevitable.

Reserves: a hope for survival?

Game reserves, if they are well policed, provide a real refuge for endangered species as places where they can live their lives free from the threat of hunters and loggers. In areas where their habitat is protected and where hunting is banned, endangered species stand a much better chance of survival. Generally, too, where they are not under pressure, species are likely to breed more successfully.

Zoos: good or bad?

Not everyone agrees that zoos should exist. The idea of keeping animals in captivity for public entertainment seems cruel and unnecessary. This was certainly a justifiable criticism of zoos in the past. However, many

A sight you're not likely to see in the wild: the Spix's macaw is now thought to be extinct in its rainforest home and lives on only as a captive species.

zoos today play a vital role in the survival of extremely rare species. In a lot of cases, the species being looked after in the world's zoos are dying out in the wild. Zoos also help to raise public awareness about the plight of endangered species, and encourage more people to get involved in conservation.

Captive breeding

Zoos can also offer captive breeding programmes, helping threatened species to

CASE STUDY

THE SPIX'S MACAW

The last known Spix's macaw in the wild (a male) disappeared from its Brazilian rainforest home in 2000. The Spix's macaw suffered from the loss of its habitat and was also targeted by the exotic pet trade. So this species, which was discovered just 150 years ago, now survives only in captivity, and not many even there. In 2000 there were thought to be a mere 54 captive Spix's macaws still living.

breed in safety. The ultimate purpose of most captive breeding programmes is to reintroduce endangered species to their natural habitats once they exist in sufficient numbers. However, captive breeding programmes have a number of issues to address:

- There needs to be a sufficiently broad gene pool to prevent inbreeding. That is, zoos must ensure that related animals do not breed with each other, as it causes weaker offspring. Zoos across the world often co-operate with each other on captive breeding programmes to ensure the gene pool is sufficiently broad.

- Where a species is being threatened by habitat destruction, and the habitat destruction continues, there may be nowhere left in the wild where the species can be reintroduced. Some argue that funds used for captive breeding programmes would be better spent helping to preserve species in their natural habitat.

- Captive-bred animals need to be nurtured in an environment as similar to their natural habitat as possible. Otherwise they are likely to be much less capable of hunting and foraging, finding shelter and avoiding predators when reintroduced to the wild.

A success story: the golden lion tamarin

The golden lion tamarin of the Brazilian rainforest was a species in severe decline. By 1993 there were just 272 left in the wild and they were classified as 'critically endangered' on the IUCN Red List. An international captive breeding programme, together with better habitat protection, has helped increase the population to over 1,000 in the wild, along with a 500-strong captive population, by 2010. One-third of the wild population is made up of reintroduced animals. The golden lion tamarin's status was downgraded to 'endangered' in 2003.

Holidays on the wild side

People's awareness of endangered species has grown over recent decades. Many of us have become interested in seeing species in their original habitats – normally inaccessible and almost untouched areas of the planet – and this has given rise to a new holiday trend, known as ecological tourism, or 'ecotourism'. Ecotourism can help endangered species to survive. If the local population can be convinced that they can make more money by allowing people to come and look at the endangered species than they can by hunting those species or destroying their habitats, then they are more likely to want to preserve them.

Some of the profits from ecotourism are fed directly into conservation work, benefiting the very species that the tourists have come to see. In many countries, ecotourism is now big business. If you are tempted to take a trip into the wilderness,

The golden lion tamarin has been brought back from the brink of extinction through good protection in the wild and successful captive breeding and reintroduction programmes.

FACTS and FIGURES

WHALE WATCHING

Whale watching is an activity that many ecotourists enjoy taking part in. In 2009 whale watching brought in US$2.1 billion worldwide and employed some 13,000 people. And its popularity is set to grow. According to forecasts, the industry could soon be worth up to US$2.5 billion and employ 19,000 people.

Source: A M Cisneros Montemayor, U R Sumaila, K Kaschner and D Pauly, University of British Colombia, 2010

it is important to check that the tour is sustainable – in other words, that your visit is not going to cause further damage to the area you want to visit.

You can help too!

As discussed in Chapter 4, climate change is creating problems for many species. So think about how you can reduce your own impact on the planet every day. Do you really need to take the car? Could you walk, cycle or take public transport instead?

You can also offer your support to conservation projects. There are plenty of charities at work helping to preserve the endangered species of the world. Some, like WWF, deal with all kinds of environmental problems. Others, like the Orang-utan Foundation, specialize in the preservation of a particular species. Use the worldwide web to find out which organizations work to support a particular species that interests you.

You can provide support by raising funds for the organizations concerned. This helps pay for their conservation and awareness-raising work. Some also offer you the opportunity to 'adopt an animal'. This means that any money you raise will go

to supporting a particular animal that the organization looks after in the wild. They will usually provide you with regular updates on the individual animal's progress.

In conclusion

There are thousands of species under threat in the world today. It is vital that young people like you learn about their plight so that the movement to preserve and protect them continues into the future. We need to learn how to treat our world in a way that does less damage. If we take too much from our planet, we may find one day that we have become the next endangered species!

Smile please! Tourists experience a close encounter with a polar bear. Ecotourism may, in future, generate the income needed to protect the species that tourists are paying to see.

Glossary

adaptation A change in structure, function or behaviour by which a species or individual improves its chance of survival in a specific environment.

background extinction rate The standard rate of extinction in earth's geological and biological history before humans became a major cause of extinctions.

bioaccumulation The accumulation of a substance, such as a toxic chemical, in the tissues of a living organism.

climate The general or average weather conditions of a certain region, including temperature, rainfall and wind.

conservation-reliant species Endangered or threatened species that require continuing human intervention to survive.

DDT Dichlorodiphenyltrichloroethane – a powerful insecticide that can accumulate in the bodies of prey species and which in high concentrations can cause hormonal changes to top predators, such as decreased fertility and reproductive problems.

deforestation The cutting down and removal of all or most of the trees in a forested area.

ecosystem A community of interacting organisms and their physical environment.

ecotourism Tourism to exotic, often threatened, natural environments to support conservation efforts and observe wildlife.

endangered species A species whose numbers are so small that the species is at risk of extinction.

endemic Native to or confined to a certain region.

extinct in the wild Describing a species in which the only known living members are in captivity.

extinction Complete destruction or annihilation.

food chain A series of organisms, each dependent on the next as a source of food.

fossil fuel A natural fuel such as coal, oil or gas, formed in the geological past from the remains of living organisms.

glacier A slowly moving mass of ice.

greenhouse gas Any of the atmospheric gases, such as carbon dioxide and methane, that contribute to global warming.

habitat The environment in which an animal or plant normally lives or grows.

hides Skins obtained from animals for human use.

ice age A period in the Earth's history when polar and mountain ice sheets spread across large parts of the Earth's surface. The most recent ice age ended about 10,000 years ago.

ice floe A mass or sheet of floating ice.

IUCN The International Union for the Conservation of Nature and Natural Resources.

ivory A substance that forms the bulk of the teeth and tusks of animals such as the elephant.

krill Small crustaceans that exist in the ocean in huge numbers. They are the main food of baleen whales.

metabolize (Of a living organism) process (the substances in food) to maintain life.

near threatened A conservation status assigned to species that may be threatened with extinction in the near future.

phytoplankton Minute, free-floating aquatic plants.

poaching Illegal hunting, fishing or harvesting of wild plants or animals.

pollution Contamination of the environment with harmful substances.

Red List The world's most comprehensive inventory of the global conservation status of plant and animal species. The Red List is compiled by the IUCN.

species A group of living organisms consisting of similar individuals that are capable of interbreeding.

symbiosis A relationship of mutual benefit or dependence.

Further Information

Books

The Earthscan Atlas: The Atlas of Endangered Species (third edition) by Richard Mackay (Earthscan, 2008)

Kingfisher Knowledge: Endangered Planet by David Burnie (Kingfisher Books, 2004)

National Geographic Investigates: Animals on the Edge: Science Races to Save Species Threatened with Extinction by Sandy Pobst (National Geographic, 2008)

100 Things You Should Know About Endangered Animals by Belinda Gallagher (Miles Kelly, 2009)

What If We Do Nothing? Endangered Species by Sean Sheehan (Franklin Watts, 2009)

Websites

www.arkive.org/
Amazing videos of endangered species to view online, plus loads of great facts.

www.iucnredlist.org
For definitive information on the state of the world's endangered species.

www.kidsplanet.org/
A very lively site with lots of information for young people.

www.wwf.org.uk
Lots of information on the state of the world's endangered species, and the work WWF carries out. A good information section for young people, too.

www.ypte.org.uk
Lots of useful resources on endangered species, extinction and climate change, written for young people and teachers.

Index

Page numbers in **bold** refer to maps and photos.